<u>KRISTALLNACHT</u>

<u>November 9-10, 1938</u>

<u>A Resource Book and Program Guide</u>

Edited and Compiled by
The Staff of the

Simon Wiesenthal Center

Published <u>on the</u>

<u>Fiftieth Anniversary of</u>

<u>Kristallnacht</u> – <u>The Night of Broken Glass</u>

"We open this session in the light of synagogue bonfires now
burning throughout Germany, and to the groans of the murdered
and cries of thousands of Jews in the concentration camps."

-Chaim Weizmann
Speaking to Zionist General Council meeting
in London as reported in **The Palestine Post**
13 November 1938.

TABLE OF CONTENTS

WHAT IS KRISTALLNACHT?

The term "Kristallnacht" ("Night of Broken Glass") refers to the organized anti-Jewish riots in Germany and Austria, November 9-10, 1938. These riots marked a major transition in Nazi policy, and were, in many ways, a harbinger of the "Final Solution."

Nazi antisemitic policy began with the systematic legal, economic, and social disenfranchisement of the Jews. This was accomplished in various stages (e.g. The Nuremberg Laws of 1935, which, among other things, stripped German Jews of their citizenship.) One of these steps involved the deportation of Polish Jews who were residing in Germany (est. 56,500). On the night of October 27, 1938, 18,000 Polish Jews were deported, but were initially refused entry into Poland by the Polish authorities. Caught in between, the Jews were forced to camp out in makeshift shelters. Upon hearing that his family was so trapped, 17 year-old Herschel Grynszpan, a student in Paris, shot the third secretary of the German Embassy, Ernst vom Rath, whom he mistook for the ambassador. This assassination served as a welcome pretext for the German initiation of Kristallnacht.

Heydrich Orders Policy of Violence

Reinhard Heydrich (the head of the Reich Main Security Office which oversaw the Gestapo, police and SD operations) sent a secret telegram at 1:20 A.M., November 10, 1938 to "all headquarters and stations of the State Police; all districts and sub-districts of the SD" He gave instructions for the immediate coordination of police and political activities in inciting the riots throughout Germany and Austria. "...The demonstrations are not to be prevented by the police," he ordered, rather, the police are "...only to supervise the observance of the guidelines."

The result of this policy was the first violent pogrom (riot) on Western European soil in hundreds of years. 36 Jews were killed (some authorities have this figure as high as 91); 30,000 more were deported to concentration camps; 267 synagogues were burned and over 7,000 Jewish shops, businesses and homes were vandalized and ransacked.

Immediately after Kristallnacht, a fine of one billion marks was levied, not upon the criminals, but upon the victims, the Jewish community of Germany. Along with the fine came a decision, taken in a conference of Nazi leaders on November 12, 1938, to "Aryanize the German economy, to get the Jew out...." Nazi policy had now moved into the overt destruction of all Jewish life in the Third Reich.

Apathy in the Western World

The violence of Kristallnacht aroused the world to condemn the Nazi actions. President Franklin D. Roosevelt recalled the American ambassador from Berlin stating that he, "could scarcely believe that such things could occur in a twentieth century civilization." However, even the condemnations failed to change western immigration policies. With a few exceptions (e.g. England, which increased its absorption of refugees after Kristallnacht), the doors to safety remained barred. As one leader of German Jewry stated two months after Kristallnacht (January 25, 1939), "From America, nothing tangible (in immigration possibilities) has arrived." With violent antisemitism now institutionalized, and with few places to flee, the Jews of Germany, Austria, and later, occupied Europe, were trapped and doomed.

Kristallnacht serves as the symbol of that destruction. The synagogues and Torah scrolls that were burned and desecrated, signified, as Rabbi Leo Baeck had earlier realized, that "the thousand-year history of the Jews in Germany had come to an end." It is that noble history and glorious legacy of German Jewry that we remember on Kristallnacht, a legacy of religious scholarship, intellectual creativity and scientific achievement. Nobel Prize winners and rabbinic scholars, businessmen and soldiers, government ministers and social activists all had their worlds shattered, along with the thousands of windows that gave Kristallnacht its name.

The Legacy of Kristallnacht

There are important lessons to be drawn from Kristallnacht, for it served as a bridge experience for both Jews and Nazis. For the Jews, there was the terrifying realization that political antisemitism can lead to violence, even in Western Civilization. It also demonstrated that apathy can still pervade the world when the lives of Jews or other minorities are threatened.

For the Nazis, Kristallnacht taught that while the world might condemn their pogroms, it would not actively oppose them. World opinion, however, taught the Nazis the value of secrecy in the perpetration of future actions against Jews. Added to the complaints of Germans offended by the random violence of Kristallnacht, the stage was set for the "Final Solution"--the organized, bureaucratically efficient genocide of 6,000,000 men, women, and children.

In retrospect, Kristallnacht was more than the shattering of windows and illusions. It portended the physical destruction of European Jewry. As such, this commemoration must be observed both as a memorial and as a warning.

DESTRUCTION OF THE SYNAGOGUES. 9 NOVEMBER 1938

Cities and towns in which one or more Synagogues were burned.

MEMORIAL PROGRAM

Reader: As we commence our memorial meeting we are
thankful to live in a democracy in which the
protection of human rights and the sanctity of
the individual is the highest ideal.

Anthem: "Star Spangled Banner" or "God Bless America"

Reader: Tonight, as we light the memorial candles for the
martyrs, we commemorate "The Night of Broken
Glass," an event that paved the way for the
destruction of European Jewry.

Instructions: To accompany the candle-lighting, recite either:
the names of six German-Jewish communities at-
tacked or major synagogues violated. (See map p.7)

A)   <u>Communities</u>
      Berlin   Frankfurt am Main
      Breslau   Mannheim
      Cologne   Vienna

B)   <u>Synagogues</u>
      Boerneplatz Synagogue (Frankfurt am Main)
      Fasanenstrasse Synagogue (Berlin)
      Heilbronn Synagogue
      Mannheim Synagogue
      Oranienburgerstrasse Synagogue (Berlin)
      Rostock Synagogue

Reader: Rabbi Leo Baeck, the great communal leader of
German Jewry, composed this prayer to be read on
the eve of Yom Kippur, 1935. The Gestapo banned
the reading of this prayer, and arrested Rabbi
Baeck. Although it was composed before
Kristallnacht, its origins and themes make it a
proud statement of German-Jewish belief in the
face of adversity.

Prayer: "At this hour the whole house of Israel stands
before its God, the God of Justice and the God of
Mercy. We shall examine our ways before Him. We
shall examine what we have done and what we have
failed to do; we shall examine where we have
gone and where we have failed to go. Wherever we
have sinned we will confess it. We will say we

have sinned and will pray with the will to repent before the Lord and we will pray: Lord forgive us!

"We stand before our God and with the same courage with which we have acknowledged our sins, the sins of the individual and the sins of the community; we shall express our abhorrence of the lie and its expressions: this slander is far below us. We believe in our faith and our future. Who brought the world the secret of the Lord Everlasting, of the Lord Who is One? Who brought the world understanding for a life of purity, for the purity of the family? Who brought the world respect for man made in the image of God? Who brought the world the commandments of justice, of social thought? In all these the spirit of the Prophets of Israel, the Revelation of God to the Jewish People had a part. It sprang from our Judaism, and continues to grow in it. All the slander drops away when it is cast against these facts.

"We stand before our God. Our strength is in Him. In Him is the truth and dignity of our history. In Him is the source of our survival through every change, our firm stand in all our trials.

"Our history is the history of spiritual greatness, spiritual dignity. We turn to it when attack and insult are directed against us. The Lord led our fathers from generation to generation. He will continue to lead us and our children through our days.

"We stand before our God; we draw strength from His Commandments, which we obey. We bow down before Him, and we stand upright before Man. Him we serve, and remain steadfast in all the changes around us. We put our faith in Him, in humility, and our way ahead is clear, we see our future.

"The whole House of Israel stands before its God at this hour. Our prayer, our faith, and our belief is that of all the Jews on earth. We look upon each other and know ourselves, we raise our eyes to the Lord and know what is eternal.

"'Behold, He that guardeth Israel shall neither slumber nor sleep.'

"'He who maketh peace in high places, may He make peace for us and for all Israel, and say ye, Amen.'

"We are filled with sorrow and pain. In silence
we will give expression to all that which is in
our hearts, in moments of silence before our God.
This silent worship will be more emphatic than
any words could be."

Reader: "What is Kristallnacht?" —A Recounting of the
                 Events

Instructions: The overview, "What is Kristallnacht?" (pp. 5-6),
                 and the fact sheet (p.14) should be used to
                 recount what occurred November 9-10, 1938.

Reader: All this took place in Germany and Austria, in
                 the heart of Western Civilization.

Song: "The Ballad of Kristallnacht" (see pp. 31-33)

Reader: The classic statement of Jewish belief in the
                 eventual redemption of the world and in the tri-
                 umph over evil is the "Ani Ma-amin", whose words
                 were on the lips of many of the martyrs of the
                 Nazi era.

Song: "Ani Ma-amin" (See p. 34)

Survivor's
 Account:

Instructions: If at all possible, it is recommended that a
                 survivor or an eyewitness of Kristallnacht de-
                 scribe his/her experience. If a survivor is not
                 available, then the account of a survivor or an
                 eyewitness could be read. Another alternative
                 would be to show film footage of Kristallnacht.
                 (See pp. 20-24 for selected personal narratives.
                 Additional accounts are in the bibliography, pp.
                 36-39.)

CIVIC PROCLAMATION

Instructions: Many communities will have civic proclamations that stress the lessons of Kristallnacht. The following format may be replicated.

WHEREAS, Kristallnacht, (The Night of Broken Glass) in Nazi Germany and Austria led to the culmination of the first period of persecution of the Jewish people, a period marked by legal disenfranchisement, social segregation, pressured emigration, and systematic exclusion from economic life

WHEREAS, Kristallnacht was a pogrom in the tradition of a long European history of violent antisemitism

WHEREAS, This pogrom was not spontaneous or even mob directed, but instigated by the state of Germany with the full cooperation of those who were sworn to protect the powerless and the weak

WHEREAS, Kristallnacht led to the death of 36 Jews; the arrest and deportation of 30,000 Jews to concentration camps; the setting afire of synagogues; the looting of 7,000 Jewish shops and businesses, and a fine of 1 billion marks levied upon the victims - the Jewish community

WHEREAS, Kristallnacht signalled the beginning of the second period of Jewish persecution: officially directed violence and murder that culminated in the "Final Solution," the destruction of the European Jewish Community, and the liquidation of 6,000,000 Jews - 1 1/2 million of whom were children;

BE IT RESOLVED that the _____ designates November 9-10, 19__ as an official day of commemoration and memory for the ____ anniversary of Kristallnacht, and the _____ also commends the teaching of mutual tolerance and understanding so as to

prevent any recurrence of
that tragic and fatal event.

Address: Suggested theme: Significance of the 50th Com-
               memoration of Kristallnacht.

Prayer: Yizkor, the memorial prayer to be followed by
               "E-1 Maleh Rachamim."

Instructions: Either the names of individuals who perished on
               Kristallnacht, or the collective term, "Kedoshim
               (Holy Martyrs) of Kristallnacht" would be ap-
               propriate for use in these prayers.

Reader: The past cannot be erased;   what was destroyed
               cannot be rebuilt; those who were murdered cannot
               be brought back.   Yet through the terrible night
               of the Shoah a beacon of hope still shone for
               many - a Jewish nation in the Land of Israel.   We
               conclude our program with this anthem of hope,
               "Hatikvah," and add to it the hope that all
               people, Jews and non-Jews, will be able to learn
               the lessons of Kristallnacht and to so avoid the
               experience of persecution and genocide.

Anthem: "Hatikvah"

The looted interior of the synagogue in Zeven (West Germany)
dumped onto the town's main square and later burned.

FACT SHEET

Date:	November 9 - 10, 1938
Sites:	Jewish communities throughout Germany and Austria
Perpetrators:	Mobs of Germans and Austrians, acting under instructions of the Nazi hierarchy
Damage:	Arrested and sent to concentration camps (Buchenwald, Dachau, Sachsenhausen): 30,000 Jews (8,000 from Austria)
Murdered:	36 Jews (other sources put this figure at 91) 36 more severely injured
Vandalized and/or set ablaze:	7500 Jewish homes and businesses 267 synagogues (76 completely destroyed)
Pretext:	Assassination of German diplomat, Ernst vom Rath, by Polish-Jewish refugee, Herschel Grynszpan, in an attempt to protest the forced deportation of his family, amongst others, to the Polish-German border.
Causes:	Nazi policy decision based on:

Causes:

1. Internal Nazi Party power struggles as segments of the party (i.e. The S.A., the propaganda section) wanted a greater role in the anti-Jewish activities

2. Urge to expedite the exclusion of Jews from German life

3. Economic factors such as the necessity to raise large amounts of money to pay for the rearmament of the German militry

4. 15th anniversary of Hitler's "Beer-Hall Putsch" of 1923 created an atmosphere that encouraged street violence

Aftermath:

1. The Jewish community is immediately fined 1,000,000,000 Reichsmarks; Nazi government confiscates all insurance claims

2. Nazis expedite plan for "elimination of the Jew from (the) economic life" of Germany established as official policy, November 12, 1938

PERSONALITIES

LEO BAECK (1873-1956)

Rabbi, leader of organized German Jewry during Nazi era. Although realizing that when the Nazis took power, "the thousand-year history of German Jewry had come to an end," he refused all offers to escape, insisting that he could flee, "only when he was the last Jew alive in Germany." He was arrested several times and finally sent to Theresienstadt, where he clandestinely taught philosophy and theology. He survived the Holocaust and died in London in 1956.

JOSEF GOEBBELS (1897-1945)

Nazi Minister of Propaganda, who organized the Kristallnacht pogrom, asserting his power and authority in internal Nazi policies.

HERMANN GOERING (1893-1946)

Commander-in-Chief, Luftwaffe, President of Reichstag, Prime Minister of Prussia and second in authority to Hitler. On November 12, 1938, he convened a conference to deal with the results of Kristallnacht, at which time heavy sanctions were imposed on the Jewish community.

HERSCHEL GRYNSZPAN (1821-19?)

17 year-old Polish Jew, living in France, who shot Ernst vom Rath upon hearing of his family's plight (deported from Germany to no-man's land between Germany and Poland). Grynszpan was arrested, never tried, and later handed over to the Nazis. His eventual fate is uncertain.

REINHARD HEYDRICH (1904-1942)

Head of Reich Main Security Office, he issued a telegram of instruction to rioters on November 10, 1938. On November 12, he participated in a meeting designed to plan the removal of Jews from German economic life. Later, in 1942, he convened and participated in the Wannsee Conference where the "Final Solution" was adopted.

ERNST VOM RATH (19? -1938)

Diplomat (Third Secretary) in the German legation in Paris. Neither particularly pro-Nazi nor important, his assassination provided the excuse for Kristallnacht.

DOCUMENTS

Heydrich's Instructions, November 1938
Riots of Kristallnacht

Secret
Copy of Most Urgent telegram from Munich of November 10, 1938, 1:20 A.M.
To:
All Headquarters and Stations of the State Police
All Districts and Sub-districts of the SA
Urgent! For immediate attention of Chief or his deputy!

Re: Measures against Jews tonight

Following the attempt on the life of Secretary of the Legation vom Rath in Paris, demonstrations against the Jews are to be expected in all parts of the Reich in the course of the coming night, November 9/10, 1938. The instructions below are to be applied in dealing with these events:

1.   The Chiefs of the State Police, or their deputies, must immediately upon receipt of this telegram contact, by telephone, the political leaders in their areas -- Gauleiter or Kreisleiter -- who have jurisdiction in their districts and arrange a joint meeting with the inspector or commander of the Order Police to discuss the arrangements for the demonstrations. At these discussions the political leaders will be informed that the German Police has received instructions, detailed below, from the Reichsfuehrer SS and the Chief of the German Police, with which the political leadership is requested to coordinate its own measures:

a)   Only such measures are to be taken as do not endanger German lives or property (i.e. synagogues are to be burned down only where there is no danger of fire to neighboring buildings).

b)   Places of business and apartments belonging to Jews may be destroyed but not looted. The police are instructed to supervise the observance of this order and to arrest looters.

c)   In commercial streets particular care is to be taken that non-Jewish businesses are completely protected against damage.

d)   Foreign citizens - even if they are Jews - are not to be molested.

2.   On the assumption that the guidelines detailed under para. 1 are observed, the demonstrations are not to be prevented by the Police, who are only to supervise the observance of the guidelines.

3.   On receipt of this telegram Police will seize all archives to be found in all synagogues and offices of the Jewish communities so as to prevent their destruction during the demonstrations. This refers only to material of historical value, not to contemporary tax records, etc. The archives are to be handed over to the locally responsible officers of the SD.

4.   The control of the measures of the Security Police concerning the demonstrations against the Jews is vested in the organs of the State Police, unless inspectors of the Security Police have given their own instructions. Officials of the Criminal Police, members of the SD, of the Reserves and the SS in general may be used to carry out the measures taken by the Security Police.

5.   As soon as the course of events during the night permits the release of the officials required, as many Jews in all districts – especially the rich – as can be accommodated in existing prisons are to be arrested. For the time being only healthy male Jews, who are not too old, are to be detained. After the detentions have been carried out the appropriate concentration camps are to be contacted immediately for the prompt accommodation of the Jews in the camps. Special care is to be taken that the Jews arrested in accordance with these instructions are not ill-treated...

Signed Heydrich,
SS Gruppenfuehrer

TELEGRAM RECEIVED

FROM

JR
This telegram must be
closely paraphrased be-
fore being communicated
to anyone. (br)

Leipzig

Dated November 10, 1938

Rec'd 8:40 a.m.

Secretary of State,

Washington.

November 10, 11 a.m.

Violent anti-Semetic ~~pogrom~~ *pogrom* in progress in

Leipzig. Three synagogues in flames one next Consulate

burning but fire under control. Hundreds of shop

windows throughout city smashed no American property or

lives molested as yet. Fur district badly damaged.

BUFFUM

HTM:DDM

TELEGRAM RECEIVED

MY
This telegram must be
closely paraphrased be-
fore being communicated
to anyone. (D)

FROM Berlin

Dated November 13, 1938

Rec'd 11:20 a.m.

Secretary of State

Washington
614, November 13, 3 p.m.

Stories of violence, ill-treatment, and arrest of Jews

during Thursday and Friday come to me hourly. Most of them

cannot be confirmed. Last night, however, I was talking

with a number of American pressmen and they told me that

realizing the gravity of the measures they had reported to

their papers only events which had been seen by them personally

or by members of their staffs. Certain of the correspondents

anticipate trouble with Goebbels but are in a frame of mind

almost to welcome it as they are more than ordinarily sure

of their facts and seething with indignation.

WILSON

JRL
KLP

U.S. CONSULAR TELEGRAMS

The Great Synagogue on Oranienburgerstrasse (Berlin)
in flames on Kristallnacht

EYEWITNESS ACCOUNTS AND REMINISCENCES

A Letter by a Firefighter

This letter was written by a retired fireman, who remembered "Crystal Night" in Laupheim (Germany).

The alarm went off between 5-5:30 A.M., and as usual, I jumped on my bicycle towards the firehouse. I had a strange feeling when I got there and saw many people standing in front of it. I was not allowed to go into the firehouse to take the engines out, or even to open the doors. One of my friends, who lived next to the Synagogue, whispered to me, "Be quiet - the Synagogue is burning; I was beaten up already when I wanted to put out the fire."

Eventually we were allowed to take the fire engines out, but only very slowly. We were ordered not to use any water till the whole synagogue was burned down. Many of us did not like to do that, but we had to be careful not to voice our opinions, because "the enemy is listening."

Only after one of the party members was worried that his house was going to catch fire, were we allowed to use water. But, even then, we just had to stand and watch until the House of Prayers was reduced to rubble and ashes.

In the meantime, the marshalls rounded up the Jews and dragged them in front of the Synagogue, where they had to kneel down and put their hands above their heads. I saw with my own eyes how one old Jew was dragged down and pushed to his knees. Then the arsonists came in their brown uniforms to admire the results of their destruction.

....Everyone seemed rather quiet and subdued... We had to stand watch at the Synagogue to make sure there were no more smoldering sparks. My turn was from 10-11 and 2-3 P.M. The brown uniforms paraded around to admire their work.

As I was watching the destroyed Synagogue and the frail old Jews, I wondered whose turn would be next!... When would it be our turn? Will the same thing happen to our Protestant and Catholic Churches!

A Personal Memoir

by Michael Bruce

Michael Bruce, a non-Jewish Englishman, provided this
eyewitness account:

...Hurriedly we went out into the street. It was crowded
with people, all hurrying towards a nearby synagogue, shouting and gesticulating angrily.

We followed. As we reached the synagogue and halted, silent
and angry, on the fringe of the mob, flames began to rise
from one end of the building. It was the signal for a wild
cheer. The crowd surged forward and greedy hands tore seats
and woodwork from the building to feed the flames.

Behind us we heard more shouts. Turning, we saw a section
of the mob start off along the road towards Israel's store
where, during the day, piles of granite cubes, ostensibly
for repairing the roads, had been heaped. Youths, men and
women, howling deliriously, hurled the blocks through the
windows and at the closed doors. In a few minutes the doors
gave way and the mob, shouting and fighting, surged inside
to pillage and loot.

By now the streets were a chaos of screaming bloodthirsty
people lusting for Jewish bodies. I saw Harrison of **The
News Chronicle**, trying to protect an aged Jewess who had
been dragged from her home by a gang. I pushed my way
through to help him and, between us, we managed to heave her
through the crowd to a side street and safety.

We turned back towards Israel's, but now the crowd, eager
for fresh conquests, was pouring down a side road towards
the outskirts of the city. We hurried after them in time to
see one of the foulest exhibitions of bestiality I have ever
witnessed.

The object of the mob's hate was a hospital for sick Jewish
children, many of them cripples or consumptives. In minutes
the windows had been smashed and the doors forced. When we
arrived, the swine were driving the wee mites out over the
broken glass, bare-footed and wearing nothing but their
nightshirts. The nurses, doctors, and attendants were being
kicked and beaten by the mob leaders, most of whom were
women.

Kristallnacht at the Dinslaken Orphanage

Reminiscences

By

Yitzhak S. Herz

At 7 A.M., the morning service in the synagogue of the institution was scheduled to commence. Some people from the
town usually participated, but this time nobody turned up.
About 7:30 A.M. I ordered 46 people - among them 32 children
- into the dining hall of the institution and told them the
following in a simple and brief address:

> As you know, last night a Herr vom Rath, a member
> of the German Embassy in Paris, was assassinated.
> The Jews are held responsible for this murder.
> The high tension in the political field is now
> being directed against the Jews, and during the
> next few hours there will certainly be antisemitic
> excesses. This will happen even in our town. It
> is my feeling and my impression that we German
> Jews have never experienced such calamities since
> the Middle Ages. Be strong! Trust in God! I am
> sure we will withstand even these hard times. No-
> body will remain in the rooms of the upper floor
> of the building. The exit door to the street will
> be opened only by myself! From this moment on
> everyone is to heed my orders only!

At 9:30 A.M. the bell at the main gate rang persistently. I
opened the door: about 50 men stormed into the house, many
of them with their coat or jacket collars turned up.   At
first they rushed into the dining room, which fortunately
was empty, and there they began their work of destruction,
which was carried out with the utmost precision.   The
frightened and fearful cries of the children resounded
through the building. In a stentorian voice I shouted:
"Children go out into the street immediately!" This advice
was certainly contrary to the order of the Gestapo.   I
thought, however, that in the street, in a public place, we
might be in less danger than inside the house. The children
immediately ran down a small staircase at the back, most of
them without hat or coat - despite the cold and wet weather.
We tried to reach the next street crossing, which was close
to Dinslaken's Town Hall, where I intended to ask for police
protection. About ten policemen were stationed here, reason
enough for a sensation-seeking mob to await the next development. This was not very long in coming; the senior police officer, Freihahn, shouted at us: "Jews do not get
protection from us! Vacate the area together with your
children as quickly as possible!" Freihahn then chased us

back to a side street in the direction of the backyard of the orphanage. As I was unable to hand over the key to the back gate, the policeman drew his bayonet and forced open the door. I then said to Freihahn: "The best thing is to kill me and the children, then our ordeal will be over quickly!" My officer responded to my "suggestion" merely with cynical laughter. Freihahn then drove all of us to the wet lawn of the orphanage garden. He gave us strict orders not to leave the place under any circumstances.

Facing the back of the building, we were able to watch how everything in the house was being systematically destroyed under the supervision of the men of law and order - the police. At short intervals we could hear the crunching of glass or the hammering against wood as windows and doors were broken. Books, chairs, beds, tables, linen, chests, parts of a piano, a radiogram, and maps were thrown through apertures in the wall, which, a short while ago, had been windows or doors.

In the meantime, the mob standing around the building had grown to several hundred. Among these people I recognized some familiar faces, suppliers of the orphanage or tradespeople, who, only a day or a week earlier had been happy to deal with us as customers. This time they were passive, watching the destruction without much emotion.

At 10:15 A.M. we heard the wailing of sirens! We noticed a heavy cloud of smoke billowing upward. It was obvious from the direction it was coming from that the Nazis had set the synagogue on fire. Very soon we saw smoke clouds rising up, mixed with sparks of fire. Later I noticed that some Jewish houses, close to the synagogue, had also been set alight under the expert guidance of the fire brigade. Its presence was a necessity, since the firemen had to save the homes of the non-Jewish neighborhood.

The New York Times.

Copyright, 1938, by The New York Times Company.

Entered as Second-Class Matter,
Postoffice, New York, N. Y.

NEW YORK, THURSDAY, NOVEMBER 10, 1938.

PP

BERLIN RAIDS REPLY TO DEATH OF ENVOY

Nazis Loot Jews' Shops, Burn City's Biggest Synagogue to Avenge Paris Embassy Aide

Wireless to THE NEW YORK TIMES.

BERLIN, Thursday, Nov. 10.—Despite authoritative warnings against anti-Jewish excesses issued before news of the death of Ernst vom Rath, Third Secretary of the German Embassy in Paris, who died there yesterday afternoon as a result of shots fired at him by a young Polish Jew Monday, violent anti-Jewish demonstrations broke out all over Berlin early this morning.

Raiding squads of young men roamed unhindered through the principal shopping districts, breaking shop windows with metal weapons, looting or tossing merchandise into the streets or into passing vehicles and leaving the unprotected Jewish shops to the mercy of vandals who followed in their trail in an unprecedented show of violence.

While crowds were still touring the streets at 7 A. M. viewing the debris left behind in all the principal shopping districts, Berlin fire-fighting forces were striving to control the burning of the city's largest synagogue, in the Fasanenstrasse, in the fashionable West End.

The fire had been set by a group of vandals and the flames soon encompassed the wooden structure. Fire-fighting units from all over the city were intent on confining the flames to the synagogue.

While large crowds watched the destruction of the building, residents in the vicinity moved their automobiles from garages in the neighborhood to safer places.

Nazi Guards Watch Vandalism

The vandalism began in the downtown shopping district on the Leipzigerstrasse and Friedrichstrasse soon after 2 A. M. As if possessing a "premonition" that something might happen groups of uniformed Elite Guards were gathered at the corner of those two streets when the demonstrators arrived.

The raiding parties for the most part were composed of youths seemingly between 20 and 30, who arrived on the scene in large open automobiles of a model frequently used by leading party officials or their guards.

Many of the raiders in the downtown districts wore boots—which are worn by all party groups when in uniform—and they worked with a precision that was a tribute to "spontaneous demonstrations."

Alighting quickly from the cars, the vandals hacked away at windows, accompanied by the laughs and jokes of onlookers. The windows were destroyed, the goods were removed from the show cases and tossed into the streets or passing vehicles, and the vandals passed on to the next jewelry shop—easily recognizable because since the last anti-Jewish demonstrations in the early Summer all Jewish-owned shops must have the name of their proprietors whitewashed on the windows in large block letters.

On the corner of the Friedrichstrasse and the Leipzigerstrasse the large department store of Arnold Mueller was an easy target. A man, a non-Jew, was observed making some protest, but he was attacked by raiders who struck him with the metal weapons and he might have been seriously injured had not members of the police and other onlookers intervened.

In the fashionable West End shopping district similar events took place. Along the Tauenzienstrasse, most of whose shops are still in Jewish possession, the attacks began soon after 3 A. M.—when night club patrons were on their way home.

Jewelry Shop Looted

The writer observed three cases of looting after raiders had broken the windows of lingerie, fur and jewelry shops. The looters waited until the raiders had passed on to the next Jewish-designated shop and then quickly grabbed something from the show windows, after which they ambled unconcernedly away.

On the Nuernbergerstrasse a man took a handful of hats from a bro-

BERLIN RAIDS REPLY TO DEATH OF ENVOY

Continued From Page One

ken shop front and walked leisurely away in full sight of three uniformed night watchmen.

In the West End large crowds followed the proceedings and were politely asked by the raiders and their accompaniers not to block the sidewalks.

However, that the onlookers were not wholly sympathetic to the proceedings was evidenced by the faces of some of them, as well as by the statements of three poorly dressed workers who at three different observation points, seeing the writer taking notes, said in different phrases but all to the same effect:

"Do not forget to write that it is not working people who are doing this."

From Munich this morning came reports of similar disorders when party veterans who were celebrating the anniversary of the 1923 beer cellar Putsch heard of Herr vom Rath's death. Added details indicated that uniformed Elite Guards and Storm Troopers urged onlookers to assist in the proceedings.

An official German News Bureau dispatch from Dresden yesterday said that "spontaneous demonstrations" against Jews had taken place there and that "police were sent to protect the Jews and despite their livid rage the masses restrained themselves, so no serious riots resulted."

There were also reports of a demonstration before the office of the official French tourist agency here yesterday afternoon, which, however, was quickly dispersed.

An Official Warning

All these demonstrations took place despite the issuance yesterday of an official German News Bureau statement following reports of the burning of a synagogue in Westphalia. The statement said:

"In informed circles it is explained, relative to demonstrations against synagogues and Jewish business houses resulting from the indignation of the population of Kurhessen following the murderous attack at the Paris Embassy, that despite all justification for this indignation authoritative quarters now as before take the stand that measures against Jews in Germany cannot occur on individual responsibility but must have legal bases.

"Official organs feel it to be their task to convince the aroused population of the necessity of comporting itself with discipline despite monstrous provocations such as that recently made from Jewish quarters in Paris."

This statement somewhat inhibited the violence of the press campaign against the Jews, but Herr vom Rath's death took precedence in the press before the commemoration ceremonies for National Socialism's "martyrs" yesterday and this most recent victim was acclaimed as one of them.

As a final honor Herr vom Rath was promoted to Embassy Counselor First Class by Chancellor Hitler, Foreign Minister Joachim von Ribbentrop.

That further legal measures against the Jews are now being prepared is asserted to be a certainty. Some reports hint at drastic capital levied. As a preliminary step rumored are current, Jewish cultural organizations and newspapers will be closed down.

The press demands not only "legal but also political expiation" for the murder, which is interpreted here as a demand on France to take action against Jewish refugees from Germany.

Chancellor Hitler telegraphed condolences to Herr vom Rath's parents in Paris. The French Chargé d'Affaires called at the Foreign Office to express his government's condolences.

C. Brooks Peters Wires The New York Times.

The New York Times.

Copyright, 1938, by The New York Times Company.

Entered as Second-Class Matter,
Postoffice, New York, N. Y.

NEW YORK, FRIDAY, NOVEMBER 11, 1938.

P

NAZIS SMASH, LOOT AND BURN JEWISH SHOPS AND TEMPLES UNTIL GOEBBELS CALLS HALT

BANDS ROVE CITIES

Thousands Arrested for 'Protection' as Gangs Avenge Paris Death

All Vienna's Synagogues Attacked; Fires and Bombs Wreck 18 of 21

Jews Are Beaten, Furniture and Goods Flung From Homes and Shops — 15,000 Are Jailed During Day—20 Are Suicides

EXPULSIONS ARE IN VIEW

Plunderers Trail Wreckers in Berlin—Police Stand Idle —Two Deaths Reported

By OTTO D. TOLISCHUS
Wireless to THE NEW YORK TIMES.

BERLIN, Nov. 10.—A wave of destruction, looting and incendiarism unparalleled in Germany since the Thirty Years War and in Europe generally since the Bolshevist revolution, swept over Great Germany today as National Socialist cohorts took vengeance on Jewish shops, offices and synagogues for the mur-

der by a young Polish Jew of Ernst vom Rath, third secretary of the German Embassy in Paris.

Beginning systematically in the early morning hours in almost every town and city in the country, the wrecking, looting and burning continued all day. Huge but mostly silent crowds looked on and the police confined themselves to regulating traffic and making wholesale arrests of Jews "for their own protection."

All day the main shopping districts as well as the side streets of Berlin and innumerable other places resounded to the shattering of shop windows falling to the pavement, the dull thuds of furniture and fittings being pounded to pieces and the clamor of fire brigades rushing to burning shops and synagogues. Although shop fires were

quickly extinguished, synagogue fires were merely kept from spreading to adjoining buildings.

Two Deaths Reported

As far as could be ascertained the violence was mainly confined to property. Although individuals were beaten, reports so far tell of the death of only two persons—a Jew in Polzin, Pomerania, and another in Bunzdorf.

In extent, intensity and total damage, however, the day's outbreaks exceeded even those of the 1918 revolution and by nightfall there was scarcely a Jewish shop, cafe, office or synagogue in the country that was not either wrecked, burned severely or damaged.

Thereupon Propaganda Minister Joseph Goebbels issued the following proclamation:

"The justified and understandable anger of the German people over the cowardly Jewish murder of a German diplomat in Paris found extensive expression during last night. In numerous cities and towns of the Reich retaliatory action has been undertaken against Jewish buildings and businesses.

"Now a strict request is issued to the entire population to cease immediately all further demonstrations and actions against Jewry, no matter what kind. A final answer to the Jewish assassination in Paris will be given to Jewry by way of

legislation and ordinance."

What this legal action is going to be remains to be seen. It is known, however, that measures for the extensive expulsion of foreign Jews are already being prepared in the Interior Ministry, and some towns, like Munich, have ordered all Jews to leave within forty-eight hours. All Jewish organizational, cultural and publishing activity has been suspended. It is assumed that the Jews, who have now lost most of their possessions and livelihood, will either be thrown into the streets or put into ghettos and concentration camps, or impressed into labor brigades and put to work for the Third Reich, as the children of Israel were once before for the Pharaohs.

Thousands Are Arrested

In any case, all day in Berlin, as throughout the country, thousands of Jews, mostly men, were being taken from their homes and arrested—in particular prominent Jewish leaders, who in some cases, it is understood, were told they were being held as hostages for the good behavior of Jewry outside Germany.

In Breslau they were hunted out even in the homes of non-Jews where they might have been hiding.

Foreign embassies in Berlin and consulates throughout the country were besieged by frantic telephone calls and by persons, particularly weeping women and children, begging help that could not be given them.

SUBSCRIPTIONS: Local: LP.2.250 a year; LP.1.250 a half year:— Foreign: £3.- a year. The rate for display advertisements is 150 mils per column inch. Other rates supplied on request. The right is reserved to make changes in wording or to decline or discontinue any advertisement or to postpone insertions when space is not available.

THE PALESTINE POST

JERUSALEM Hassolel Road P. O. Box 81, Telephone 4233
Tel Aviv - Jaffa: 65 Allenby Road, P. O. Box 1125, 'Phone 4251-4252.
Haifa: Khayat Square, opposite the Post Office entrance, P.O.B. 66, 'Phone 1990.

FRIDAY NOVEMBER 11 1938 JERUSALEM VOL. XIV. No. 3797 PRICE 10 MILS

NAZI HOOLIGANS VENT WRATH ON THE JEWS THROUGHOUT GERMANY

DEATH OF ATATURK

Creator of Modern Turkey Passes Away at 58

GENERAL INEUNU MAY SUCCEED

ANKARA, Thursday (R). The death took place this morning of Kemal Ataturk, President of the Turkish Republic, at the age of 58.

Abdul Halik Renda, the President of the National Assembly, has assumed the interim Presidency, and the Assembly will elect a new President at 11 o'clock tomorrow morning.

General Ineunu, ex-Premier and for many years Ataturk's right-hand man, is the most likely candidate.

Kemal Ataturk fell ill of a serious liver disease early this year and his condition become grave at the beginning of August last, when seven doctors were in attendance on board his private yacht near Istanbul.

He seemed to be recovering when, on October 18, a relapse set in. Ataturk, however, again showed remarkable vitality and was reported on October 23 to be better.

TURN FOR WORSE

This week, however, his condition took a further turn for the worse, and last night he was reported to have lapsed into a coma. From hour to hour, Turkey waited for news of his condition; and a bulletin issued at 1 o'clock (G.M.T.) last night stated that general weakness was affecting his heart.

Special precautions seemed to have been taken to prevent the news of his death, which took place early this morning, from being known before midday. It was then said that he had died peacefully.

The Lieutenant Who Became President

If ever a man was marked out for greatness and high position in the life of his people, it was Mustapha Kemal, the lowly Army lieutenant who rose to be President of an Asiatic Republic born out of the stress of war and post-War flux; and if ever a man deserved the title of Father of Modern Turkey, it was the first secular Head of State in many hundreds of years of dynastic rule.

Mustapha Kemal or, as he was known in later years, Kemal Ataturk (Great Turk), was born in Salonica in 1880, son of a minor Turkish customs official. Brought up and educated by his mother, a woman of character and ability, young Mustapha entered a military school, where he proved an exceptional student, especially in Mathematics; and his teacher gave him the distinctive surname of "Kemal" (an Arabic word for perfection).

In 1904 he was gazetted lieutenant but, on the same day, was arrested for political intriguing and banished to Damascus where, a year later, he founded the secret political society "Vatan" ("Fatherland").

LIFE AT JAFFA

From Damascus he was transferred to Jaffa and thence made his way secretly to Salonica to organize a similar political movement in the European provinces of Turkey. The society he founded was afterwards affiliated to the Young Turks' Committee of Union and Progress.

After an attempt to re-arrest him, he was forgotten and in 1907 was promoted to a Captaincy and sent to Salonica, where he resumed his revolutionary activities. In 1914 he was appointed Colonel.

When the Great War broke out, he was among those who believed in Germany's ultimate defeat and was not particularly in favour at Turkish H.Q. But he was placed in charge of the Dardanelles defences, and inspired the resistance to the British attack.

Sent to the Caucasus, he was promoted Pasha and fought the Russians successfully. In 1917 he was posted to the Hedjaz and, in the same year, was appointed to command the Seventh Army Corps, under General von Falkenhayn, who was endeavouring to recover Baghdad.

COMMAND IN PALESTINE

After protesting against German military tactics and refusing the commands of the Second and Seventh Corps, he ultimately agreed to take the Seventh Corps command in Palestine in 1918, but it was when Turkish hopes were lost. He kept together the remnants of his corps on the retreat following General Allenby's great victory, and before the end of September was appointed Commander-in-Chief of all the forces constituting the so-called "Yilderim" group.

He opposed the policy of complete surrender at Mudros (October 30, 1937), and retired from activity, but when the Greeks landed at Smyrna in May, 1919, he accepted the Inspector-Generalship of the XIth. Corps. Resuming his political activity, he convened congresses at Erzerum and Sivas in 1919 and secured endorsement of his programme to fight for national existence to the bitter end.

NATIONAL ASSEMBLY

On April 23, 1920, he gathered together the Nationalist members of the Turkish Parliament who had fled from Constantinople and was unanimously elected President of the new National Assembly.

During the summer campaign of 1920-21, the supreme crisis of the Greco-Turkish war, he was appointed generalissimo of the Turkish forces by the National Assembly, and after the battle of Sakaria was given the rank of Field Marshal (at 41) and the traditional title of "Ghazi" (the Victor).

On October 29, 1923, the Republic was proclaimed following the abdication of the Sultan and the abolition of the Caliphate. The National Assembly unanimously elected him first President and in practice, if not in theory, he became Dictator. On November 1, 1927, he was unanimously re-elected.

Kemal was author of "Die Nationale Revolution, 1920-27" (1928) and "Die Neue Turkei, 1919-27" (1929).

MODERNISATION

The history of his rule from 1923 to 1938 was a continuous story of the modernisation of Turkey. He abolished the fez in favour of European headgear; forbade women to wear the veil; introduced the European calendar, and compulsory education; and introduced Latin characters for Turkish. He endeavoured unceasingly to bring Turkey into line on an equal footing with Western Powers, and ruthlessly stamped out all Levantinism in the character of the Turkish people.

A powerful Navy and Army, a pact with Great Britain, friendship for Russia, modern buildings, a five-year Industrial plan, prosperous trade, social hygiene and other public amenities in his own country were part of the achievements which remain as a monument to his untiring industry for his country.

LONDON PRESS FAVOURS TALKS

GOVERNMENT MUST NOT FORGET IDEA OF NATIONAL HOME

LONDON, Thursday (Palcor & R). Although most of this morning's newspapers refrain from discussing the prospects of the London discussions with representatives of Jews and Palestinian Arabs, as well as of neighbouring Arab states, there is general agreement that, in summoning a conference in a supreme effort to achieve agreement, the British Government has acted wisely.

NO CRITICISM

"The Times" says editorially:

"No criticism can be levelled with any semblance of justice against the Government's decision to promote a conference of Jewish and Palestinian Arab delegates.

"A settlement by consent of the Jewish-Arab quarrel would instantly relieve this country of serious anxieties, and soon restore peace and prosperity to the Holy Land whose inhabitants, all except the professional banditti, desire to see a speedy end to the present period of disorder and uncertainty.

DEBATABLE POINT

"In any case, such a conference would have an inestimable advantage of giving the Jews and Arabs alike, the certainty that the Government would give a fair hearing to their respective cases.

"The most debatable point in the Government's statement is the decision to invite neighbouring Arab States to send their delegates to the Conference."

The editorial recalled that the interference by Arab rulers in 1936 was regarded in Great Britain and by the League of Nations as undesirable and embarassing.

Referring to Plan C. the article pointed out, "It reduces the Jewish State to microscopic dimensions, leaving out the successful colonies studding the Plain of Esdraelon. It would certainly have been rejected by the Jews, giving the Arabs an excellent opportunity of resisting the policy without concession.

"Fortunately, Plan C. was not adopted by the Government, which based its rejection on economic and financial reasons."

The article regarded it as ironic that, while the Commission admitted that the increase of Jewish immigration had led to improved life within the Arab population and that Palestine had become a paying concern only by the investment of Jewish capital, this should at the same time be an obstacle to the fulfilment of Jewish ambitions.

"MUST NOT FAIL"

"The News-Chronicle," in welcoming the Government's decision, said that the time was ripe for making a supreme effort to bring about an understanding between Jews and Arabs, and the conference deserved every good wish.

"If the Conference fails, the Government will have no recourse but to apply their own solution and enforce it firmly. But the conference must not be allowed to fail."

...

BRITAIN'S POLICY

While more critical of the Government's past handling of the Palestine question, "The Manchester Guardian" regards the Conference with satisfaction, but adds that the Government must not forget that the policy of England is based on the Balfour Declaration and on the idea of a National Home of which less and less has been heard since the days of the Peel report.

(Other London Press Comment on Page 2. Palestine Press Reaction and Jewish Agency Statement on Page 8.)

AFTER MIDNIGHT

The burning of synagogues and the demolition of Jewish stores continued last night throughout Germany. Shops were destroyed from Koenigsberg far in the northwest to towns in the southeast of the Reich. Looting was in full swing in the West End of Berlin last night.

Answering charges of underproduction of aircraft, Sir Kingsley Wood stated yesterday in the House of Commons during the debate on defence deficiencies that next year's Air Estimates would probably be £200,000,000, or £80,000,000 more than this year.

When the Prime Minister was asked to give an assurance in the House of Commons yesterday that the Government would not transfer any British colonies or Mandated territories to other Powers, he declined to add to his previous statements, and refused to be drawn by further questions.

Negotiations with Arabs and Jews on Basis of the Mandate

STATEMENT IN HOUSE ON FORTHCOMING TALKS

LONDON, Thursday. — Replying to a question by Major Attlee in the House of Commons this afternoon in reference to representation at the London conference on Palestine, Mr. Malcolm MacDonald said that the Government was in a communication with the Governments of Egypt, Iraq, Saudi-Arabia, the Yemen and Trans-Jordan.

It was not proposed to invite the Mufti of Jerusalem as his record over many years made him wholly unacceptable as an Arab representative in London.

The Opposition Leader asked the Colonial Secretary to bear in mind the need for adequate representation of the poorer Arabs and Jewish labour.

PRELIMINARY TALKS

Answering supplementary questions, Mr. MacDonald declared that the Government would enter the Palestine Discussions bound by obligations to both Jews and Arabs under the Mandate, but it would not seek to prevent either party from presenting its arguments for the modification of the Mandate. Mr. MacDonald added that the Government would watch the situation very carefully.

He made it clear that the preliminary discussions in London would be between:

(1) The Arabs of neighbouring countries and the British Government;

(2) The representatives of the Jewish Agency and the British Government.

The discussions, he thought, might well develop into a three-party conference. The conferences would be in the form of purely informal discussions and there was no question of voting.

It was suggested also that invitations might be sent to the United States of America, Poland and Rumania, among others. Mr. MacDonald declined to do so, but stated that if any question arose of the treaty rights of the United States being involved, the Government would enter into immediate discussions with the United States.

In his reply to Major Attlee the Colonial Secretary said:

"As was announced in the Statement which His Majesty's Government published yesterday, it is proposed to invite representatives of the Palestine Arabs and of neighbouring states on the one hand, and of the Jewish Agency on the other. With regard to neighbouring states, we are in communication on the matter with the Governments of Egypt, Iraq, Saudi-Arabia and the Yemen, as well as Trans-Jordan.

CONTACT WITH FRENCH

"Other territories which, by reason of their contiguity, are interested in the Palestine question, are Syria and the Lebanon. They are under French Mandatory control and consequently stand on a different footing. It is not proposed that the representatives of these territories should be invited to the discussions, but His Majesty's Government intend to keep closely in touch with the French Government and to keep them informed of any developments which may be of interest to Syria and the Lebanon.

"With regard to the representation of the Palestine Arabs, I am in consultation with the High Commissioner and I am not at present in a position to indicate what arrangements will be made.

"The House will have observed that the Government reserve the right to refuse to receive leaders whom they regard as responsible for the campaign of assassination and violence. His Majesty's Government must exercise this right in the case of the present Mufti of Jerusalem, whose record over many years makes him wholly unacceptable. With regard to others, I can add nothing at present. The matter must depend on the position in Palestine.

RESTORING PEACE

"His Majesty's Government made it clear in the Statement which they issued yesterday that they will continue their responsibility for the Government of the whole of Palestine. Their ultimate aim is to give lasting peace and prosperity to the people of the country. Their immediate duty is to establish law and order throughout the land.

"They earnestly hope that they will secure the cooperation of the peoples of Palestine, Jews and Arabs alike, in promoting that state of peace which is so essential for the success of the policy of negotiation which has been announced.

"The Arabs in Palestine are now offered an opportunity of coming to London, in company with the representatives of neighbouring countries, to enter into free and full discussions on the problem of Palestine with His Majesty's Government.

"In these circumstances, His Majesty's Government will expect that rebellious activities should be brought to an end. If they do not cease, His Majesty's Government must continue to take all such measures as may be necessary to put an end to disorders."

NO NEGOTIATIONS WITHOUT LEADERS

The Inter-Parliamentary Palestine Congress delegation (Arab) at present in London has issued a statement declaring that to negotiate about Palestine in the absence of her accredited leaders would not give an authoritative or permanent character to any settlement.

Moslems and Arabs everywhere genuinely desired to be on good terms with Great Britain, said the statement, and the delegation requested the Government not to allow the present opportunity to be spoiled by false notions of prestige.

COST OF TROOPS

LONDON, Thursday (R). — Mr. MacDonald in the course of a written reply in the House of Commons revealed that the extra cost of maintaining Army units in Palestine over and above the cost of maintaining them in their normal stations in 1938-39 was estimated to be £1,700,000.

It was not possible to furnish figures of the total cost of the military forces in Palestine, but the additional cost of the Air Force was over the normal expenditure for 1938-39 to date by £11,000.

COUNTRYWIDE POGROMS

SYNAGOGUES RAZED TO THE GROUND; SHOPS WRECKED, LOOTED

BERLIN, Thursday (R). Since the early hours of this morning, there have been vehement systematic and organized attacks on and destruction of Jewish property in various parts of Germany, shops and synagogues being wrecked and gutted by arson.

The new outburst of anti-Jewish feeling followed the death of Herr von Rath, who is being brought to Frankfurt-on-Main (his native town) tomorrow for a State funeral.

This afternoon, the German Propaganda Minister, Dr. Joseph Goebbels, issued a proclamation calling for an immediate cessation of the attacks on Jewish property, and said that sufficient expression had been given to the German protest.

FRESH DECREES

Reprisals must now stop, and the final answer to the Jews would take the form of fresh legislation and decrees, he declared.

The demonstrations broke out in Munich last night at the conclusion of the three-day anniversary celebrations by the "Old Guard" of the abortive Munich bierhalle "putsch" in 1923.

Almost every Jewish shop in Munich was wrecked, and the sole remaining synagogue was razed to the ground. All Jewish males under 60 were placed under arrest.

The campaign spread this morning to the rest of Germany and Austria, where whole Jewish districts were raided.

In Vienna, only one synagogue escaped destruction by fire. Two were blown up, and several others set on fire. Some 5,000 Jews were arrested, 22 Jews committed suicide this morning, and all Jews waiting outside the British Consulate for emigration visas were taken into custody.

Nine synagogues were burned in Berlin alone, and the fires were got under control only at a late hour. Jewish shop-windows, sometimes as far up as the third storey, were shattered or smeared with slogans, and goods flung into the street.

NO POLICE CONTROL

In the afternoon, gangs of hooligans broke into West End Berlin shops smashed windows and threw the goods inside out into the street, where there were frantic rushes to secure fur, shoes and other articles in the confusion. During the day, said foreign observers, Kurfurstendam littered with glass, wreckage and goods, gave the impression that there had been an air raid or a big explosion.

The Police made no effort to check the hooliganism and smashing of windows, but only controlled the traffic. Crowds of sightseers on foot, in private cars and taxis, thronged the streets.

Foreign observers in Munich and Berlin said that the crowds were mostly silent, and did not approve of what had

(Continued on Page 2)

U.S. Republicans Again In the Running

77 SEATS GAINED IN HOUSE OF REPRESENTATIVES

NEW YORK, Thursday (R). — Republican gains in the United States elections have been much larger than expected, with 77 seats in the House of Representatives and eight in the Senate. Further results are still to be declared.

In the State Governorships, Republicans obtained 17 and Democrats 15, and the distribution now is:— 30 Democrats and 18 Republicans.

Republican and other Conservative elements are predicting a substantial Opposition in future to "New Deal" measures in Congress, and while they are talking optimistically concerning the Presidential election of 1940, Democratic circles are inclined to minimize the effect in this respect.

A SETBACK

Observers differ about the extent to which the election results may be regarded as a setback for President Roosevelt. Supporters of the "New Deal" say that some of the successful Republican candidates were more in sympathy with the "New Deal" than some of the Democrats. On the other hand, Democrats elected came from the Conservative wing.

It is thought that the tendency of the elections was a movement towards moderate liberalism. One thing is clear, — the Republicans are again in the running after having been eclipsed for several years.

ROYAL VISIT

It is officially announced in London that Their Majesties will sail on the cruiser, Repulse, to visit Canada and the United States. The Repulse will be escorted by a cruiser squadron.

The date of the sailing has not yet been fixed, but Reuter understands that Their Majesties will arrive in Canada about the middle of May.

ONLY FEW INCIDENTS REPORTED IN QUIET DAY

There were few incidents throughout the country reported yesterday.

There was a reaction in Tulkarm following the engagement at Irtah village on Wednesday when 19 bandits were killed, and a shop strike was declared yesterday.

An immediate Curfew was imposed on Jaffa as from 7 o'clock yesterday morning, after Mr. Rachwolsky, an employee of the Posts and Telegraphs Department was shot and slightly wounded by an unknown assailant when entering the Post Office. The Curfew was lifted at 4 p.m.

The following reports are taken from the Public Information Officer's bulletin issued yesterday:

BOMBS AND SHOTS AT MILITARY

Two Arab houses were demolished by troops in Nablus yesterday following the throwing of a bomb at the Brigade Headquarters in the town on Wednesday night.

A second bomb was thrown at the military billet at dawn yesterday, but failed to explode.

Military and police billets in Gaza were also the targets of snipers on Wednesday night. There were no casualties, and the fire was returned.

GAZA STATION FIRE

At 10 o'clock yesterday morning a railway trolley was set on fire by unknown persons, in Gaza Railway Station. The flames were extinguished by the Fire Brigade.

Shots were fired at Hefzibah settlement (Haifa District) during Wednesday night, but there were no casualties.

TREES DESTROYED

A small number of eucalyptus trees was uprooted in Rosh Pinah settlement on Wednesday.

Two hundred and fifty orange trees were cut down in a grove in Rishon-le-Zion on Wednesday. The damage is estimated at about LP. 450.

The same afternoon a police car overturned at Km. 24 on the Frontier Road, and two Arab constables were slightly injured.

PASSENGER CUT BY GLASS

Yesterday morning shots were fired at long range at traffic on the Coastal Road near Taba village. One shot broke the window of a car and a Jewish passenger was slightly cut by broken glass.

INJURED SOLDIERS

The names of the soldiers injured in the ambush of a railway trolley near Kalkilya on Wednesday are Lance-Corporal J. Mackintosh; Private A. Easton, Private J. Cairns, and Private A. H. Burton. All the men, who were seriously wounded, belong to the Royal Scots Regiment.

SUBSCRIPTIONS: Local: LP.3.250 a year; LP.1.550 a half year; Foreign: £3. a year. The rate for display advertisements is 150 mils per column inch. Other rates supplied on request. The right is reserved to make changes in wording or to decline or discontinue any advertisement or to postpone insertions when space is not available.

THE PALESTINE POST

JERUSALEM Hassolel Road P. O. Box 81, Telephone 4233

Tel Aviv - Jaffa: 65 Allenby Road, P. O. Box 1125, Phone 4251-4252.

Haifa: Khayat Square, opposite the Post Office entrance, P.O.B. 66, Phone 1390.

SUNDAY NOVEMBER 13 1938 JERUSALEM VOL. XIV. No. 3798 PRICE 10 MILS.

NEW NAZI SAVAGERY SPELLS DOOM OF JEWISH LIFE IN GERMANY

MILITARY AND POLICE ACTION IN SEARCHES

TWELVE KNOWN ARAB CASUALTIES IN 3 DAYS

Military and police operations throughout the country during the past three days included searches in eight different localities.

One member of his Majesty's Forces was killed and three were injured in various localities.

Three Jews have been wounded, and 12 Arabs known to have been killed or wounded including a small girl, as a result of terrorism and military action since Thursday.

PLANE FORCED DOWN

When an R.A.F. machine cooperating with the military in an engagement at Beit Furik village east of Nablus, made a forced landing the pilot, Sergeant Pilot Tebbs, was seriously hurt, while Corporal George Wickens, of the Green Howards, was slightly injured in the same engagement in which heavy casualties were inflicted on the band.

Many arrests were made as a result of these searches, and over a thousand rounds of ammunition seized together with several rifles, bombs and detonators, some documents and a camera.

Shots were fired yesterday afternoon at troops who were on duty at a Traffic Control Post in the Bab Zeitun Quarter of Gaza. One British soldier was killed and another severely wounded. A 24-hour curfew was imposed as from 3 p.m.

EXPLOSION KILLS FIVE

An explosion which occurred on Thursday night in the house of Khalil el Awoor in Al Majdal, north of Gaza, completely wrecked the building, killing the owner and four other persons.

Yesterday afternoon a party of British police in a tender were fired on near Jenin police station. They returned the fire and killed an Arab who was subsequently found to be in possession of a rifle and more than 250 rounds of ammunition.

CUSTOMS GUARD SHOT DEAD

Yesterday afternoon a customs guard named Abdul Hafiz of Kalkania was shot dead by unknown assailants while walking in the Nazareth Road, Haifa.

An Arab of Kabatiya village, Samaria, Nasser el Kassem was shot

(Continued on Page 2)

AFTER MIDNIGHT

A decree was issued in Paris last night providing for the revaluation of the gold stock in the Bank of France at the rate of 170 francs to the £. Gold is now valued about 110 francs to the £. Another decree provides that agricultural production be nationalised by agreements to be reached between the parties concerned.

"We shall solve the political Catholic problem with the same consequences as the Jewish question," declared Gauleiter Jury, the Regional Leader of Lower Austria, in addressing a Nazi meeting yesterday in Gaenserndorf.

"A BLACK DAY FOR GERMANY" – TIMES

BRITISH PRESS CONDEMN NAZI OUTRAGES

LONDON, Saturday (R. and Palcor).— The entire British press devotes space today to the riots and pillaging of Jewish houses and businesses in Germany. Comment takes the form of unprecedentedly strong condemnation, even in journals 'friendly' to Germany.

"The Times" heads its editorial with the words "A Black Day for Germany" and states that no amount of foreign propaganda could have done Germany so much harm as the events which have taken place. Similar views are expressed by other leading morning papers.

CRUELTY AND DESTRUCTION

The Archbishop of Canterbury in a letter to "The Times," expresses the feeling of indignation with which he claims Christians in Britain have "read of the deeds of cruelty and destruction which were perpetrated last Thursday in Germany and Austria."

Adding that whatever provocation may have been given by the deplorable act of a single irresponsible Jewish youth, reprisals on such a scale, so fierce, cruel and vindictive, could not possibly have been justified.

Dr. Lang calls for the remembrance in prayers offered in Churches tomorrow of those who have suffered in this fresh onset of persecution.

Sir Archibald Sinclair, leader of the Liberal Party, in a speech last night said that the treatment of the German Jews was Germany's business only so long as she did not expel them after having robbed them.

Sir Archibald said that the refugee problem must be tackled in a general spirit, and that in the light of recent events British obligations towards the Jewish National Home must be interpreted in a generous spirit.

NAZI ARMS FOR ARABS

He said that the Arabs who were incited by German and Italian propaganda, and aided by German arms, should not be allowed to frighten the British Government from fulfilling its pledges towards the Jewish National Home. He insisted that there was room in Palestine for the Jews, and that the Arab complaints were unreasonable since Jewish immigration had helped development, and the Jews must find a home.

The Foreign Under-Secretary, Mr. R. A. Butler, yesterday received a deputation consisting of Mr. Neville Laski, Chairman of the Board of Jewish Deputies, and Mr. C. G. Montefiore, President of the Anglo-Jewish Association, together with Mr. L. H. Glueckstein, M.P.

PILLAGED OF 84 MILLION POUNDS TO "PAY" FOR MURDER OF GERMAN OFFICIAL

BERLIN, Saturday (R).—Jews in Germany have been ordered to pay one milliard marks (over 80 million pounds sterling) as compensation for the murder of Herr von Rath, the secretary of the German Embassy in Paris.

The indemnity will be levied in the form of a special tax on all Jewish property. Since this property is officially valued at about 10 milliard marks, the tax will be at a rate of ten per cent.

MINISTERS' CONFERENCE

The decision was taken at a conference presided over by Field-Marshal Goering, attended by Dr. Frick, Reich Minister of the Interior, Dr. Goebbels, Minister of Propaganda, Dr. Guertner, Minister of Justice, and Count von Krosigk, the Minister of Finance.

Furthermore, all the damage "caused through the indignation of the people over the agitation by international Jews, on November 8, 9, and 10" must be made good by Jewish occupiers or Jewish businessmen, while sums derived from insurance companies will be confiscated for the benefit of the Reich.

The official communique which announces these decisions also contains the announcement that "further drastic measures for driving the Jews out of Germany's economic life and the elimination of provocative conditions will shortly be taken, in the form of laws and decrees." It is stated that "a number of the most drastic measures will be taken," the first of which have already been announced.

ELIMINATION PROCESS

From January 1, 1939, Jews will not be allowed to engage in
retail trade,
export businesses,
commercial offices or
independent handicraft businesses, and
will not be permitted to occupy managerial posts.

The decree forbidding Jews to own weapons is implemented by new measures announced today.

Further, a decree was issued by Dr. Goebbels, forbidding Jews to visit theatres, concerts, cinemas, music halls, dance entertainments, museums and exhibitions of any kind.

It was stated by Dr. Goebbels that there was no reason why Jews should visit such entertainments or exhibitions since they had their own cultural organizations. The activities of the latter have however been brought to a complete standstill, as all Jewish theatre, concert and cinema performances have been prohibited.

Jewish schools and newspapers have been closed down.

Ruin

EFFECT OF NEW DECREE

(By Our Commercial Correspondent)

The decree ordering Jews in Germany to pay a milliard Reichsmarks and the decision to levy this amount in the form of a ten per cent capital tax clearly reveals the intention to destroy whatever economic assets are left to the Jews.

The execution of this decree means irreparable ruin for every Jewish business in Germany and this apart from the order forbidding Jews to engage any longer in retail trade, since it is normally impossible for owners of businesses to raise ten per cent of their capital in cash.

Landlords, shopkeepers and security holders will thus be compelled to sell their property or shares, provided they can find buyers. To sell buildings has become extremely difficult. The market value is not taken into account, and the price is fixed by an "arbitrator," usually appointed by the Nazis.

In the case of securities the market has contracted to such an extent owing to forced investments in Government securities that small sales inevitably lead to heavy drops in prices. What will happen when large blocks of securities are suddenly offered for sale can readily be imagined.

Altogether the decrees amount to nothing less than the complete spoliation of what property still remains in Jewish hands.

PARIS, Saturday (R). — The funeral service for Herr von Rath took place here today at the Lutheran Church in the German Colony.

The French Foreign Minister, M. Bonnet, was present, and the Government, the President, and the President of the Chamber, were represented.

JEWS HIDING IN BERLIN WOODS

REPORTS OF TORTURE AND MURDER

LONDON, Saturday (R). — Mass arrests of Jews are still the order of the day in Berlin and other German towns. It is estimated that several thousand Jews were arrested in Berlin, while thousands, according to a report received here, are hiding in the woods round Berlin.

In Frankfort-on-Main all Jewish men between the ages of 18 and 60 were arrested and herded into concentration camps, where, like all other Jewish internees, they will have to pay for their own board and lodging, as well as for that of those Jews among them who are without funds.

Further to the demonstrations which took place on Tuesday, Wednesday and Thursday, it is now learned according to reports received here, that the worst disorders occurred in small towns where the entire population took part in smashing and looting Jewish shops. Warnings were published in the local newspapers that anybody who failed to take part would be regarded as an enemy of the regime.

QUESTION IN HOUSE

Notice was given today by Mr. Attlee, Leader of the Opposition, of a question regarding the events in Germany. This fact has caused reports in the German press that Parliament is to debate the riots.

German newspapers react to this report with an outburst of abuse, several stating that if Parliament is to debate the position of the Jews in Germany, the Reichstag will be called to debate British policy in Palestine.

TORTURED TO DEATH

A leading personality who witnessed some of the scenes in Berlin and arrived here yesterday (reports Palcor), stated that no Jewish business was left intact and many Jewish houses were damaged and looted. Scores of Jews, according to him, were not only beaten but literally tortured to death.

Officially it is stated in Berlin that a Polish Jew was killed in Munich, where 1,400 Jews are now stated to have been arrested, over half of whom were brought to Dachau concentration camp.

The announcement that one Jew was killed was made in Munich today by the Gauleiter, Herr Wagner, at a mass meeting. This accident occurred, he said, "because he could not keep his mouth shut."

Herr Wagner also expressed satisfaction that the last synagogue in Munich had now finally been got rid of. "I hope foreigners of all kinds in Munich will now keep out of our affairs," said Herr Wagner.

ATTACK ON CATHOLICS

In another part of his speech he attacked the Roman Catholic Church which he accused of giving shelter to the Jews. Following his speech a mob went to the palace of Cardinal Faulhaber, known as an opponent of the regime, and smashed a number of windows.

Only brief and casual reports of the disturbances were published in the German press. The Berlin streets were cleaned overnight, and apart from paneless windows and closed shops there was nothing yesterday to remind passers-by of the demonstrations. The damage in Berlin alone is estimated at tens of millions of marks.

The Zionist Organization's Offices in Berlin were destroyed by a mob and leading Zionists were arrested.

ONE HUNDRED JEWS FLEE PERSECUTION

LONDON, Saturday. — One hundred Jews, men, women and children, from Germany and Austria sailed from Liverpool last night in the Canadian Pacific liner, Duchess of Bedford, for Montreal on their way to Australia and New Zealand.

All the men are skilled workers and all have received permits to enter the Dominions. Some had sufficient means to pay their fares. Others have been assisted by Jewish Aid Societies.

Some of the women had to leave their husbands in Germany, because they had not enough money for both fares.

RECOGNISES ITALY'S CONQUEST

CAIRO, Saturday (R). — Egypt has decided to recognise the Italian conquest of Abyssinia. An announcement to this effect was made here today.

GEN. INUENU NEW TURKISH PRESIDENT

REGARDED AS ATATURK'S LOGICAL SUCCESSOR

ISTANBUL, Saturday (R).— General Ismet Inuenu, former Prime Minister and close collaborator of Kemal Ataturk, was unanimously elected President of the Republic by the National Assembly in Ankara today.

Following the election, a reshuffle of the Cabinet was announced.

Dr. Rushdi Aras, the Foreign Minister is replaced by the former Minister of Justice, Shukru Aracaghu, while the Minister of the Interior, M. Shukru Kaya is replaced by the former Minister of Health, Refik Saydan.

Dr. Aras has held the post of Foreign Minister continuously since 1925, and was a well-known figure at Geneva where he represented Turkey since she became a member of the League in 1932.

The new President of Turkey was born in 1882 and served a distinguished career in the Army, before joining the Nationalist movement led by Kemal in 1919 and taking over command of the army that defeated the Greeks.

He represented Turkey at the Lausanne Conference in 1923 where she was finally recognised by the former Allied Powers.

In 1925 Inuenu became Prime Minister, a post he occupied for 12 years. He was then known as Ismet Pasha.

His resignation last year was reported to have been due to differences of opinion with the President on Turkey's foreign policy, but his unanimous election is proof that he continues to be regarded as the logical successor to Kemal Ataturk.

In connection with the death of Kemal Ataturk, the Turkish Consulate in Jerusalem on Friday received visits from members of the Consular Corps, including the Consuls of Iran, Iraq and Yugoslavia.

Mr. L. Kohn and Mr. E. Epstein called on behalf of the Jewish Agency and Mr. E. Elmaleh on behalf of the General Council of Palestine Jews.

The latter has also telegraphed to the new President of the Turkish Republic expressing the sorrow of Palestine Jewry on the news of the death of Kemal Ataturk.

The Chief Rabbinate of Palestine has sent the following message signed by Chief Rabbi Herzog and Rabbi Meir to the Prime Minister of Turkey:

"Palestine Jewry's profoundest sympathy and condolence with Turkish nation in serious loss sustained through untimely death of great leader and regenerator of Turkey, Gazi Kemal Ataturk."

INSURGENTS RAID BARCELONA

BARCELONA, Saturday (R). — Barcelona was raided today by Insurgent planes which dropped a number of bombs in the centre of the town. The number of casualties is stated to have been very small.

Fighting on land is progressing, though neither side reports progress on the Segre front. On the Ebro, the Republicans are still defending much of the ground taken in their successful July offensive.

"WE OPEN OUR SESSION TO THE LIGHT OF SYNAGOGUE FIRES"

WEIZMAN OVERCOME WITH EMOTION AT GENERAL ZIONIST MEETING IN LONDON

LONDON, Saturday (Palcor). Meeting under the shadow of the tragic events in Germany, the session of the Zionist General Council opened here at 11 o'clock yesterday morning in the presence of 73 delegates from all parts of the world, including the United States and Palestine.

The Council observed the two minutes' silence customary on Armistice Day, prior to Mr. Ussishkin opening the meeting with a tribute to the victims of the Palestine disturbances, to Dr. F. Rottenstreich and to Mr. L. Motzkin, on the occasion of the fifth anniversary of his death.

Recalling the desecration of the Wailing Wall, Mr. Ussishkin went on to describe the happenings in Europe during the last few days and closed with an appeal for unity.

"Reality overcomes all internal differences," he said, "let us unite for the sole salvation of the Jewish people which is Palestine."

U. S. JEWS THANKED

Mr. Ussishkin paid a special tribute to the Jews of America for their recent great efforts which would not be forgotten in Zionist history. Acting on his suggestion the conference decided to send a telegram of congratulation to Mr. Justice Brandeis on the occasion of his 83rd birthday.

In a hushed silence, Dr. Weizman began his opening address with a reference to the losses recently suffered by the Jews in Palestine, among whom he named with particular sorrow the son of his colleague, Dr. Mossinsohn.

"NO PEACE" — WEIZMAN

Proceeding, Dr. Weizman said that while millions of people of all nations celebrated the Armistice today, there was no peace for the Jews. "We open this session in the light of synagogue bonfires now burning throughout Germany and to the groans of the murdered and cries of thousands of Jews in the concentration camps," he said.

Dr. Weizman was overcome by emotion and a few moments passed before he was able to continue. They had been trying, he said, during the last few days, to influence persons whom them believed to be powerful, but their efforts had been in vain.

They had obtained sympathy but they were unable to do anything. The forces of shameless cruelty could not be checked.

Zionists were not accustomed, however, to weep and wail, he said. The world in which they had been brought up when justice prevailed was breaking up, but there were still elements which justified the view that ultimately the forces of darkness would be withstood, not only so far as the Jews were concerned but for the whole world.

Dr. Weizman then referred to the Palestine situation and said that the partition scheme had been dropped, though they had not been responsible either for its presentation or for its withdrawal. The establishment of a Jewish State would have been impossible now, even if the report of the Partition Commission had been favourable, because the enemies of the Jewish people and of justice were too strong at the moment.

CYNICAL DOCUMENT

He had rarely seen a more cynical document than the Woodhead report, and he was unable to understand the mentality of its members with the exception of one who seemed to possess human feelings. The Report aimed at breaking up what the Jews had already acquired with superhuman effort.

The so-called Jewish State was apparently to be charged with the financial upkeep of the Arabs and British States which were admittedly unable to maintain themselves. Altogether the Report was a sign of the times and significant of the way in which small nations were being treated, of which Czechoslovakia was an example.

The Report, however, was now dead and ignored by the Government. The worst fears which had existed among the Jewish people for several weeks had not materialised

This was to be attributed to the dignified and courageous stand of the Jewish community in Palestine, which, he stated would remain as glorious as the struggle of the Maccabeans, second only to the united efforts of the Jews all over the world, especially in the United States, where Jews had manifested an unexampled unity and reacted to the danger in a manner which was a consolation — if consolation was possible in these days.

MANDATE IN FORCE

Dr. Weizman stressed the fact that the Balfour Declaration and the Mandate were still in force, but they were entering a period of difficulties in continuing and maintaining their work. The central theme of the immediate struggle was the question of immigration, which continued although in a thin stream.

They had received an invitation to negotiate with the Arabs, which they did not wish to refuse, but negotiations were possible only on the basis of the Balfour Declaration and the Mandate.

Concluding, Dr. Weizman said that although the project of a Jewish State had been temporarily dropped, he was convinced that it would come up again in due course. In the meantime Jewry must unite in strengthening the Jewish position in Palestine and its only instrument, the Zionist Organization.

After the close of Dr. Weizman's address, the meeting adjourned until tonight, when Mr. Shertok will give his address which will be followed by the political discussion.

SPEECH DELIVERED IN COLOGNE SYNAGOGUE 9 November 1978

A Plea for Honesty and Tolerance

by Helmut Schmidt, former Chancellor, West Germany

Mr. Federal President
Dear citizens of Cologne,
Dear Jews, Christians and Free-Thinkers in Germany,

The German night, whose observance after the passage of forty years has brought us together today, remains a cause of bitterness and shame. In those places where the houses of God stood in flames, where a signal from those in power set off a train of destruction and robbery, of humiliation, abduction and incarceration - there was an end to peace, to justice, to humanity. The night of 9 November 1938 marked one of the stages along the path leading down to hell...

GUIDELINES FOR DISCUSSION

The following guidelines are suggested for use in exploring the issues raised by Kristallnacht. They can be expanded or adapted, as the situation requires:

What led to Kristallnacht?

1. Explore the systematic discrimination against Jews that was a basic plank of Nazi policy.

2. Consider the heritage of anti-Jewish violence that existed in European society as well as the libeling and stereotyping of Jews.

3. Take into account all of the above in an assessment of the total group; evaluate the response of German and Austrian mobs on Kristallnacht.

What was new and significant about Kristallnacht?

1. Kristallnacht marked the shift from the legalized anti-Jewish discrimination symbolized by the Nuremberg Laws (which stripped German Jews of citizenship) to the outright violence of vandalism, arson, destruction, physical injury and even death, caused by the mobs of rioters.

2. Historically, Kristallnacht also marked a radical shift. For the first time in recent history, antisemitic violence was organized and incited on an official level by a Western European state.

3. Furthermore, Kristallnacht was the first pogrom in Western Europe in hundreds of years. Its occurrence in the heart of culture, removed the veneer of civilization, exposing a core of violent racism.

Kristallnacht as a "bridge experience"

1. Although violence against Jews was verbally condemned, no concrete sanctions (economic or political) emanated from the nations of the world. Thus, in effect, violent antisemitism was encouraged.

2. However, because there was verbal condemnation, and because some German sensibilities were offended, the random violence of Kristallnacht was translated into the organized, bureaucratic "Final Solution" with killing centers ultimately removed to the more isolated areas of Eastern Europe.

3. Thus, there were no more "crystal nights" in Nazi Germany, but, without Kristallnacht, there could not have been a "Final Solution."

THE BALLAD
OF CRYSTAL NIGHT

Words by Peter Wortsman

Music by Shoshana Kalisch

pain   Till it's your own face that's burned;   Till it's your own face that's

burned.   Too late to make a-mends, my friends,   Too

late,   my sto - ry ends.____

My folks came from Vienna
Forty years ago,
Said it was a cultured town—
Where'd all the culture go?
I only heard the echo.
I don't know.

Oh, the fine old-fashioned doctors
Knew all there was to learn:
The same men could recite their Greek
And watch the fires burn,
Burn, and thank God
It's not their turn.

'Twas the ninth night of November
Nineteen thirty-eight:
Skies aglow with fire
And the crowd aroused with hate.
Did you sleep well, old Vienna?
It was late.

They broke into the temples,
They broke into the stores.
So well behaved, good friends and neighbors
Double-locked their doors.
Oh, it's just the Jew.
What else is new?

Now, friends, I look around me—
I see nobody's learned.
Seems there's no way to feel the pain
Till it's your own face that's burned.
Too late to make amends,
My story ends.

Ani Mamin   אֲנִי מַאֲמִין

Ani-Mamin (I Believe)

Ani-mamin, Ani-mamin, I believe, I believe,
I believe with reassuring faith,
He will come, he will come,
I believe Messiah, he will come.
I believe, although he may delay,
I believe he'll come, Ani-mamin.

Ani mamin, ani mamin,
Ani mamin —
Beemuno shleymo
Bevias hamoshiakh.
Bevias hamoshiakh ani mamin
Veaf al pi sheyismameya
Im kol-ze ani mamin.

אֲנִי מַאֲמִין, אֲנִי מַאֲמִין,
אֲנִי מַאֲמִין —
בֶּאֱמוּנָה שְׁלֵמָה
בְּבִיאַת הַמָּשִׁיחַ,
בְּבִיאַת הַמָּשִׁיחַ אֲנִי מַאֲמִין.
וְאַף עַל פִּי שֶׁיִּתְמַהְמֵהַּ,
עִם כָּל־זֶה אֲנִי מַאֲמִין.

EPILOGUE

The tragedy of Kristallnacht was not the destruction. No nation
has been free of violence. No nation has been free of the row-
diness of the ignorant. The tragedy, rather, was that government, which should protect the individual and his property
against violence, in this instance encouraged and abetted the
violence against the Jews. The violence was a joint act by the
government and the populace. Early on the day of November 9 a
message went out from Gestapo headquarters: "There will be very
shortly in Germany actions against the Jews, especially against
the synagogues. These actions are not to be interfered with."

- Leonard Baker

RESOURCES AND BIBLIOGRAPHY

by Adaire Klein

"THE COURAGE TO REMEMBER"

The Simon Wiesenthal Center's unique poster series, a visual narrative offering new insights into the Holocaust and based on the Center's traveling exhibit, is now available. Forty full-color panels with nearly 200 original photographs, created by Wiesenthal Center researchers and historians, comprise a compelling series of posters to be used by libraries, schools, community centers, synagogues, churches and other interest groups.

Particularly appropriate for the commemoration of Kristallnacht or Yom Hashoah (Holocaust Remembrance Day), for educational and commemorative programs, these 26" x 42" posters may be wall-mounted, displayed on easels, set up in classrooms or framed as a permanent exhibit.

Available from the Simon Wiesenthal Center, Office of the Director, 9760 W. Pico Blvd., Los Angeles, CA 90035, (213) 553-9036. (Set of 40 panels: $500.00)

Bibliography

American Jewish Yearbook, v. 41 (Philadelphia: Jewish Publication Society of America, 1939-40.) pp. 261-268.

Arad, Yitzhak, Yisrael Gutman and Abraham Margaliot. Documents on the Holocaust. (Jerusalem: Yad Vashem, 1981.) pp. 102-117.

Baker, Leonard. Days of Sorrow and Pain: Leo Baeck and the Berlin Jews. (NY: Macmillan, 1978.) pp. 200-238.

Ball-Kaduri, K.Y. "The Central Jewish Organizations in Berlin During the Pogrom of November 1938 ('Kristallnacht')." In Yad Vashem Studies, v.3. (Jerusalem: Yad Vashem, 1959.) pp.261-281.

Bauer, Yehuda. A History of the Holocaust. (NY: Franklin Watts, 1982.) pp. 98-112.

Dawidowicz, Lucy S. The War Against the Jews. (NY: Seth Press, 1986.) pp. 99-106.

Eisenberg, Azriel. Witness to the Holocaust. (NY: The Pilgrim Press, 1981.) pp. 84-91.

Encyclopaedia Judaica, v.10. (Jerusalem: Keter Publishing, 1972.) "Kristallnacht," pp. 1263-1265.

Freeden, Herbert H. Grist to God's Mill. (London: Godfrey & Stephens, 1947.) Novel based on Kristallnacht.

Friedman, Saul S. No Haven for the Oppressed. (Detroit: Wayne State University Press, 1973.) "The Wagner Bill," pp. 84-88.

Front Page Israel. (Jerusalem: Palestine Post, Ltd., 1979.) pp. 48-49.

Gilbert, Martin. The Macmillan Atlas of the Holocaust. (Phila. And NY: Jewish Publication Society of America and Macmillan Publishing Co., 1982.) pp. 26-28.

Gross, Kenneth. "Anniversary of a Night too Horrible to Forget: Newsday. (Long Island, NY) 10 October 1983.

Gurwillig, Eric. "The Night of Broken Glass." Newsview. (Jerusalem) 15 November 1983.

Herz, Yitzhak S. "Kristallnacht at the Dinslaken Orphanage: Reminiscences." In: Yad Vashem Studies, v.11. (Jerusalem: Yad Vashem, 1976.) pp. 344-368.

The Holocaust: A Study of Genocide. (NY: Board of Education of the City of New York, Division of Curriculum and Instruction, 1979.) pp. 26-27; 285-290.

The Holocaust: Selected Documents in Eighteen volumes. Intro. by John Mendelsohn. (NY: Garland Publishing, 1982.) v.3: "The Crystal Night Pogrom."

Kalisch, Shoshana and Barbara Meister. Yes, We Sang! Songs of the Ghettos and Concentration Camps. (NY: Harper & Row, 1985.) pp. 29-34.

Kochan, Lionel. Pogrom. November 10, 1938. (London: Andre Deutsch, 1957.)

Legters, Lyman H. Western Society After the Holocaust. (Boulder, CO: Westview Press, 1983.) pp. 39-106.

A Letter by a Firefighter. Available: Simon Wiesenthal Center Library/Archives, Los Angeles, CA.

Lochner, Louis P. What About Germany? (London: Hodder and Stoughton, 1943.) pp. 177-190.

Loewy, Ester E. Crystal Night: A Personal Memoir. Available: Simon Wiesenthal Center Library/Archives, Los Angeles, CA.

Loewy, Ester E. Es Brent - The City is Burning. A Personal Memoir. Available: Simon Wiesenthal Center Library/Archives, Los Angeles, CA.

Lookstein, Haskel. Were We Our Brothers' Keepers? The Public
    Response of American Jews to the Holocaust. (NY: Hartmore
    House, 1985.) pp. 35-80.

McKale, Donald. "A Case of Nazi 'Justice' - The Punishment of
    Party Members Involved in the Kristallnacht, 1938." Jewish
    Social Studies. 1973, 35 (3/4) 228-238.

Milton, Sybil. "Images of the Holocaust." Holocaust and
    Genocide Studies. (vol. 1, no. 1, 1986) 27-61. Has
    several reproductions of Kristallnacht photographs.

Morse, Arthur D.   While Six Million Died: A Chronicle of
    American Apathy. (NY: Random House, 1968.) "1938: The
    Night of Broken Glass," pp.221-240.

Murray, Michelle. The Crystal Nights. (NY: Dell Publishing,
    1973.) Young Adult novel.

Nation. 25 January 1938.

New York Times. 10 November 1938, Sec. 1, p. 1; 11 November
    1938, Sec. 1, p.1.

Newsweek. 21 November 1938.

Oppenheim, Ruth. "Kristallnacht How It Was." Moment. (April
    1985) 50-54.

Peters, C. Brooks. "Reminiscences of Kristallnacht." (1978)
    Audio Cassette.   Available: Simon Wiesenthal Center
    Library/Archives.

Peters, C. Brooks. Simon Wiesenthal Center "Testimony to the
    Truth." (1987) Video Cassette. Transcript is available.

Posner, Louis. Simon Wiesenthal Center "Testimony to the
    Truth." (1988) Video Cassette.

Rabbinic Responsa of the Holocaust Era. (NY: Schocken Books,
    1985.) pp. 54-65.

Racial, Religious and Political Minorities. A Debate in the
    House of Commons, 21.11. 1938. (London: Woburn Press,
    1938.)

Roizen, Ron. "Herschel Grynszpan: The Fate of a Forgotten As-
    sassin." Holocaust and Genocide Studies. (vol. 1, no. 2,
    1986) 217-228.

Schleunes, Karl A. The Twisted Road to Auschwitz: Nazi Policy
    Toward German Jews 1933-39. (London: Andre Deutsch, 1972.)
    pp. 214-254.

Shirer, William. The Rise and Fall of the Third Reich. (NY:
    Simon & Schuster, 1960.) "The Week of the Broken Glass,"
    pp. 430-437.

Stadtler, Bea. "Young Memories of Nazis." The Jewish Advocate.
    (Boston, MA) 3 November 1983.

Thalmann, Rita and Emmanuel Feinermann. Crystal Night, 9-10
    November 1938. (NY: Holocaust Library, 1974.)

Time Magazine. 21 November 1938; 28 November 1938.

Vishniac, Roman. A Vanished World. (NY: Farrar, Straus &
    Giroux, 1983.) pp. 172-175; "Commentary on the Photo-
    graphs," last page.

Zimmels, H. J.   The Echo of the Nazi Holocaust in Rabbinic
    Literature. (NY: KTAV Publishing, 1977.) pp. 25-35.

SOURCES *

PAGE

Frontispiece: Simon Wiesenthal Center Archives 86-097A

page 7:   The Macmillan Atlas of the Holocaust, by Martin Gi
                   bert. p. 27; map 20.

pages 8-10:   Days of Sorrow and Pain, by Leonard Baker. pp. 20
                   207.

page 13:   Leo Baeck Institute, New York.

pages 16-17:   Documents on the Holocaust, ed. by Yitzhak Arad, e
                   al. pp.102-104.

page 18:   National Archives and Records Administration, Washin
                   ton, D.C. Reprinted: The Holocaust, vol. 3: "The Cry
                   tal Night Pogrom." pp. 173-174.

page 19:   Yad Vashem Archives of the Destruction, No. 213C01.

page 20:   Simon Wiesenthal Center Library/Archives.

page 21:   Days of Sorrow and Pain, by Leonard Baker. pp. 23
                   232.

pages 22-23:   Yad Vashem Studies, vol. 11. Selections from pp. 34
                   368.

page 28:   The Bulletin of the Press and Information Office
                   the Government of the Federal Republic of German
                   No. 1/vol. 6. Bonn. 3 January 1979.

pages 31-33:   Yes We Sang! Songs of the Ghettos and Concentration
                   Camps, by Shoshana Kalisch and Barbara Meister. p
                   31-34.

page 34:   We are Here: Songs of the Holocaust, compiled
                   Eleanor Mlotek and Malke Gottlieb. (NY: Education
                   Department of Workmen's Circle and Hippocrene Book
                   1983.) p.76

page 35   Days of Sorrow and Pain, by Leonard Baker. p. 230.

* Complete bibliographical information is provided in "Resources a
Bibliography." (See pp. 36-39.)

ACKNOWLEDGMENTS

The Simon Wiesenthal Center gratefully acknowledges the publishers, archives and authors, noted in the "Sources" (p. 40), for permission to reproduce their materials in this guide.

This resource guide has been edited and compiled by:

Aaron Breitbart
Adaire Klein
Rabbi Daniel Landes
Francine Lis
Dr. Gerald Margolis
Mark Weitzman

Special assistance was provided by:

Bari Kaplan
Lydia Triantopoulos

SIMON WIESENTHAL CENTER

The Simon Wiesenthal Center, established in 1977, has become the largest institution of its kind in North America dedicated to the study of the Holocaust and to the monitoring and combatting of contemporary antisemitism throughout the world. To serve its membership of nearly 370,000 families, the Center, which is headquartered in Los Angeles, also maintains offices in New York, Chicago, Miami, Jerusalem, Toronto, and Paris and is represented by legal counsel in Washington, D.C.

The Center closely interacts on an ongoing basis with public and private agencies, meeting with members of Congress, government officials, foreign diplomats, and heads of state. Among the issues addressed by the Center are the persecution of Nazi war criminals, worldwide antisemitism, neo-Nazi and other extremist movements, human rights, terrorism, and genocide.

The Wiesenthal Center is dedicated to the preservation of the memory of the Holocaust through education and awareness, with the goal that no people shall ever again fall victim to an atrocity of such magnitude. To this end, aided by the library, archives and research department, the Center has developed innovative programs, films, exhibits and publications in the areas of Holocaust Studies, Educational Outreach and Soviet Jewry.

For more information contact:

Headquarters
9760 W. Pico Blvd.
Los Angeles, CA 90035
(213) 553-9036

EASTERN REGION
342 Madison Ave.
Suite 320
New York, NY 10017
(212) 370-0320

MIDWEST REGION
320 N. Michigan Ave.
Suite 1005
Chicago, IL 60601
(312) 704-0024

SOUTHERN REGION
13400 Biscayne Blvd.
Suite 208
North Miami, FL 331
(305) 944-4500

CANADIAN OFFICE
8 King St. East
Suite 204
Toronto, Ontario M5C1B5
(416) 864-9735

ISRAEL OFFICE
Efraim Zuroff, Dir.
P.O. Box 365
Jerusalem, Israel 91003
(02) 931-586

EUROPEAN OFFICE
Paris
FRANCE

WASHINGTON, D.C.
Martin Mendelsohn
Legal Counsel